Also by James Schuyler

ALFRED AND GUINEVERE
(a novel)

FREELY ESPOUSING

A NEST OF NINNIES
(a novel—with John Ashbery)

MAY 24TH OR SO

SALUTE

THE PICNIC CANTATA
(with Paul Bowles)

THE
CRYSTAL
LITHIUM

THE
CRYSTAL
LITHIUM
by
James
Schuyler

**RANDOM
HOUSE
New
York**

The following poems originally appeared in:
The Paris Review: The Dog Wants His Dinner,
Running Footsteps, The Crystal Lithium, The Trash Book,
"Used Handkerchiefs 5¢."
Best & Co: Empathy and New Year, The Cenotaph, Part Three.
Adventures in Poetry: An East Window on Elizabeth Street,
Scarlet Tanager, Alice Faye at Ruby Foo's, Buildings,
A Sun Cab, Closed Gentian Distances.
The New Yorker: Evening Wind, Light From Canada, Blue.
The World Magazine: Light Blue Above, After Joe
Was at the Island, In Earliest Morning, A Stone Knife,
Janis Joplin's Dead: Long Live Pearl, Eyes, The Night,
Like Lorraine Ellison, Letter to a Friend: Who is Nancy
Daum?, Letter Poem #2, We Are Leaves, Await,
Steaming Ties, Watching you, Letter Poem #3, Wonderful World.
A Sun Cab: Gulls, September, The Cenotaph, Parts One and Two.

Published in the United States by
Random House, Inc., New York,
and simultaneously in Canada by
Random House of Canada Limited, Toronto.

Library of Congress Cataloging in Publication Data

Schuyler, James.
      The crystal lithium.

      Poems.
      I. Title.
PS3569.C56C7   811'.5'4   72–2326
ISBN 0–394–48144–5 (hardbound)
ISBN 0–394–70782–6 (paperbound)

Manufactured in the United States of America
by Kingsport Press, Inc. Kingsport, Tenn.

**for
Bob**

Contents

* ix

*

* x
*

Southampton
and
New York

Empathy and New Year

"A notion like that of empathy
inspires great distrust in us,
because it connotes a further
dose of irrationalism and mys-
ticism."—LÉVI-STRAUSS

Whitman took the cars
all the way from Camden
and when he got here
or rather there, said,
"Quit quoting," and took the next
back, through the Jersey meadows
which were that then. But
what if it is all, "Maya,
illusion?" I
doubt it, though. Men are not
so inventive. Or
few are. Not knowing
a name for something proves nothing. Right
now it isn't raining, snowing, sleeting, slushing,
yet it is
doing something. As a matter of fact
it is raining snow. Snow
from cold clouds
that melts as it strikes.
To look out a window is to sense
wet feet. Now to infuse
the garage with a subjective state
and can't make it seem to
even if it is a little like
What the Dentist Saw

a dark gullet with gleams and red.
"You come to me at midnight"
and say, "I can smell that after
Christmas letdown coming like a hound."
And clarify, "I can smell it
just like a hound does."
So it came. It's a shame
expectations are
so often to be counted on.

New Year is nearly here
and who, knowing himself, would
endanger his desires
resolving them
in a formula? After a while
even a wish flashing by
as a thought provokes a
knock on wood so often
a little dish-like place
worn in this desk just holds
a lucky stone inherited
from an unlucky man. Nineteen-sixty-
eight: what a lovely name
to give a year. Even better
than the dogs': Wert
(". . . bird thou never . . .")
and Woofy. Personally
I am going to call
the New Year, Mutt.
Flattering it
will get you nowhere.

Awake at four and heard
a snowplow not rumble—
a huge beast
at its chow and wondered
is it 1968 or 1969?
for a bit. 1968 had
such a familiar sound.
Got coffee and started
reading Darwin: so modest,
so innocent, so pleased at
the surprise that *he*
should grow up to be *him*. How
grand to begin a new
year with a new writer
you really love. A snow
shovel scrapes: it's
twelve hours later
and the sun that came
so late is almost gone:
a few pink minutes and
yet the days get
longer. Coming from the
movies last night snow
had fallen in almost
still air and lay
on all, so all twigs
were emboldened to
make big disclosures.
It felt warm, warm

that is for cold
the way it does
when snow falls without
wind. "A snow picture," you
said, under the clung-to
elms, "worth painting." I
said, "The weather operator
said, 'Turning tomorrow
to bitter cold.' " "Then
the wind will veer round
to the north and blow
all of it down." Maybe I
thought it will get cold
some other way. You
as usual were right.
It did and has. Night
and snow and the threads of life
for once seen as they are,
in ropes like roots.

Poem

for Trevor Winkfield
December 26, 1970

The wind tears up the sun
and scatters it in snow.
The sky smiles and out
of its mouth drifts free
a milk tooth which of itself
glides under the pillow
of a cloud. The Tooth Fairy
knows where to look and when
to lock away the leaves
long since packed up and
left: "I'm southbound." Not
now, though this funny
fluffy winter rain coasts
down and coats the grass
dry and white, a corn meal
shampoo. "Brush it in,
brush it out." Easier
said than done. Things
take the time they take:
leaves leaving, winter
and its flakes, not less
though shorter lived.

In January

after Ibn Sahl

The yard has sopped into its green-grizzled self its new year
    whiteness.

A dog stirs the noon-blue dark with a running shadow and dirt
    smells cold and doggy

As though the one thing never seen were its frozen coupling
    with the air that brings the flowers of grasses.

And a leafless beech stands wrinkled, gray and sexless—all bone
    and loosened sinew—in silver glory

And the sun falls on all one side of it in a running glance, a
    licking gaze, an eye-kiss

And ancient silver struck by gold emerges mossy, pinkly
    lichened where the sun fondles it

And starlings of anthracite march into the east with rapid jerky
    steps pecking at their shadows

Blue

for Yvonne Jacquette

beautiful New
York sky harder
so much than
soft walls you
see here around
it shadowy lamp
lighted plaster
smoothed by a hand
wielded trowel and
roller painted
by hand: Puerto
Rican blue pressed
tin ceiling sky
up into and on
which a white cup
(more of a mug)
falls, falls up-
ward and crack
splits into
two glazed
clay clouds

Spring

snow thick and wet, porous
as foam rubber yet
crystals, an early Easter sugar.
Twigs
aflush.
A crocus
startled or stunned
(or so it looks: crocus
thoughts are few) reclines
on wet crumble
a puddle of leas. It
isn't winter and it isn't spring
yes it is the sun
sets where it should and
the east
glows
rose. No.
Willow.

In Earliest Morning

an orange devours
the crusts of clouds and you,
getting up, put on
your daily life
grown somewhat shabby, worn
but comfortable, like old jeans: at the least,
familiar. Water
boils, coffee
scents the air
and level light plunges
among the layering boughs of a balsam fir
and enflames its trunk.
Other trees are scratched
lightly on the west.
A purposeful mutt
makes dark marks
in blue dew. The day
offers so much, holds
so little or is it
simply you who
asking too much take
too little? It is
merely morning
so always marvelously
gratuitous and undemanding,

freighted with messages
and meaning: such
as, day
is different from the night
for some; see
the south dazzle
in an effulgence
thrown out by an ocean;
a myriad iridescence
of green;
the shape
of the cold egg
you break
and with a fork
again break
and stir and pour
into a pan, where it lightly hisses.
The sediment
in your mind sinks
as something rises
in it, a thought
perhaps, like a tree when it
is just two green
crumpled bits of tape
secured to grit; a
memory—beyond
a box of Gold Dust
laundry soap a cherry
in full flower and
later full of fruit;
a face, a name
without a face,

water with a name:
Mediterranean, Cazenovia, or
iced, or
to be flushed
away; a
flash of
good humor, no
more than a
wink; and the sun
dims its light
behind a morning
Times of cloud.

An East Window on Elizabeth Street

for Bob Dash

Among the silvery, the dulled sparkling mica lights of tar roofs
lie rhizomes of wet under an iris
from a bargain nursery sky: a feeble blue with skim milk
    blotched
on the falls. Junky buildings, aligned by a child
("That's very good, dear") are dental:
carious, and the color of weak gums ("Rinse and spit"
and blood stained sputum and big gritty bits
are swirled away). Across an interstice
trundle and trot trucks, cabs, cars,
station-bound fat dressy women
("I never thought I'd make it")
all foundation garments and pinched toes. I don't know how
it can look so miraculous and alive
an organic skin for the stacked cubes of air
people need, things forcing up through the thick unwilling air
obstinate and mindless as the glorious swamp flower
skunk cabbage and the tight uncurling punchboard slips
of fern fronds. Toned, like patched, wash-faded rags.
Noble and geometric, like Laurana's project for a square.
Mutable, delicate, expendable, ugly, mysterious
(seven stories of just bathroom windows)
packed: a man asleep, a woman slicing garlic thinly into oil
(what a stink, what a wonderful smell)
burgeoning with stacks, pipes, ventilators, tensile antennae—

that bristling gray bit is a part of a bridge,
that mesh hangar on a roof is to play games under.
But why should a metal ladder climb, straight
and sky aspiring, five rungs above a stairway hood
up into nothing? Out there
a bird is building a nest out of torn up letters
and the red cellophane off cigarette and gum packs.
The furthest off people are tiny as fine seed
but not at all bug like. A pinprick of blue
plainly is a child running.

Alice Faye at Ruby Foo's

1 from 9 is 8
and 4 from 5 is 1
K '59
a black green and white catalog from Germany
on my desk proclaims
that 18 this December's ago (when
almost any night they might just bomb
the Hotel Henry Hudson elevator ladies
who clucked because young men were "just boys")

2

well, like I say
the chicken lady
no not in *Freaks* that was Olga
whosis Baclanava the real one
Alice Faye (glycerined feathers
humped in a rooster arch
above her butt and O those dancing shoes
stout but sporty)
dined one night in mink
blond pink and furry
or maybe just imagined it was she?

3

" 'Driver,' this lady says, 'do I
have to ride with *this*?' So what do you think
it's right beside her on the seat
and all the time I think this navy
guy is hugging up his wife.
Me, I got a heart big as a ship.
But that lady. She was burned."

4

White New York, and tin,
home of viscous egg drop soup, the red
baked banana, tasty yam and split persimmon,
out of the Annual Winter Guide of Uglifacts
a charm, like consulting Constella
in The News for fun and the oracle is apt:

Alice Faye

smiling and smiling in the flaming night

or, THINK AMERICAN
"dozing," as Cocteau said, "into her beard of orchids"

Don't be a goddess
Alice Faye, a democratic hoofer
a bosomy good sport
all good joes aspire to

O taxi cabs. O Ruby Foo.

Buildings

Buildings embankment parkway grass and river
all those cars
all those windows
each building shooting (straight up)
out of its small allotment
all those buildings fibered together
their flowing sap
traffic threading
the shark tooth city
O coral reef
O slick and edible matter
housed in seashell buildings
the most delicately leaved trees
on a high terrace waving
the most finely possible knotted net
of shadow on an incinerator shaft
sifting each evening its soot
in the violent atmosphere
in which white gulls are black
sickling a harvest of rinds
among swollen oceanic beauties
tugs nuzzle and badger
in the shatter surface salt river harbor
O morning light on dirty windows
sharpening the sepulchral church steeple
whitened by pigeons

the money insulated by limestone
and shining red granite reflects
such extraordinarily well dressed people
from among all of you
one can choose at a time only one
a woman striding the ragged grass
her fixed stare devouring the restless river
striding on the far side of the parkway
all those cars
all those millions of windows

Wonderful World

for Anne Waldman
July 23, 1969

"I," I mused, "yes, I," and turned to the fenestrations of the night beyond one of Ada and Alex Katz's windows. Deep in Prince Street lurked thin sullen fumes of Paris green; some great spotty Danes moved from room to room, their tails went whack whack in a kindly way and their mouths were full of ruses (roses). Flames in red glass pots, unlikely flowers, a spot of light that jumped ("Don't fret") back and forth over a strip of moulding, the kind of moulding that spells low class dwelling—I, I mused, take no interest in the distinction between amateur and pro, and despise the latter a little less each year. The spot of light, reflected off a cup of strong blue coffee, wasn't getting anywhere but it wasn't standing still. They say a lot of gangsters' mothers live around here, so the streets are safe. A vast and distant school building made chewing noises in its sleep. Our Lady of someplace stood up in a wood niche with lots and lots of dollar bills pinned around her. The night was hot, everybody went out in the street and sold each other hot sausages and puffy sugared farinaceous products fried in deep fat ("Don't put your fingers in that, dear") while the band played and the lady in the silver fox scarf with the beautiful big crack in her voice sang about the young man and how he ran out in front of the stock exchange and drank a bottle of household ammonia: "Ungrateful Heart." Big rolls of paper were delivered, tall spools of thread spun and spelled, Jacquard, Jacquard. Collecting the night in her hand, rolling its filaments in a soft ball, Anne said, "I grew up around here," where, looking uptown on summer evenings, the Empire State Building rears its pearly height.

Scarlet Tanager

May 13, 1967

"—in the big maple
behind the willow—"
a jet with limp spring greens
lance-like, or the head of a pike
and there it flies
and there it sits
the tanager, the bright spot
in the sunny rather evil day
the red touch green
cries out for—the soldier
in "Storm at Castelfranco."
And the drums beat
in East 95th Street
for soldiers in a storm
no, it's only a parade.
A huge and sullen Buddha
of a man waits at the starting
with his sign DOWN WITH DOVES
kids cry cadence and a bunch
of thick short men in little hats
that announce them vets
of the War to End War
(It Floats, They Laughed, Chu Chin Chow)
look defiant at those

who go counter to them
though merely strolling home.

A couple of men jump
out of the sky
wearing flags. Someone
"described as a bystander"
gets tarred and feathered.

Embittered object of our anxious
and unworthy fears, the scapegoat
in a getup like a grackle
that a cat drags in. Glorious day
in May when by the window
a wistaria hangs its violet lights
creased with a sunny pallor
and other birds than tanagers—
fluffy balls of fluffy dung—
flit to a skirl of bagpipes
in undefoliated yards
between backs of rows of houses
and men with faces like happy fists
march in well-remembered but unpracticed step
—who would study
to forget?—or is it habit, merely,
like LOOK BEFORE YOU TURN—
waving little flags, why then why then
it's hard not to believe the marchers
march for the fun of marching
to an inward tune like Mahler's happy
happy children's song
                    drums   drums

A Sun Cab

goes by below
reflected across the street
in a window
four stories up
a train
sends up its
passing metal roll
through grills and gone
the more than daily Sunday

CRIMINAL NEW JERSEY
THIRSTING FLESHPOTS OF NEW YORK

buzz
horns hums and voices
a plane unravels from the Delft
a mohair thread
torn paper shadows,
dry cool and gritty
laid on
buff gray-white and pink
    The dog in its
sunspot sleep
cries in a few fine high whimpers
drips of rain

in dust on glass
paint drops

FIDGET BALLS
FOR AN UPTIGHT
GENERATION

Shadows
fling out their feet
and step into sun
palpable and out
and motes of
who knows what
go by
up and out
of sight   Pale cornice
brokenly lighted
by light reflected
from the sunny side
a cab crosses
the sun
near the end of a street
to the river
unheard unseen
a fluent presence

The
Island

Light Blue Above

Light blue above, darker below, lightly roughened by the stirring air and with smooth tracks on it. There goes Reynald Hardie's lobster boat, taking a colorful load of pleasure-seeking shoppers to Camden.

O Air
the clear, the soot-bearer, the unseen that rips
that kills and cures, that keeps
all that is empty filled, the bright invisible

into which we move like fingers into gloves
that coats our rolling home with the sweet softness
between grape and grape skin

in silent laughter in a glass pushed down
into a basin at retreating puzzled water
constrained to rise elsewhere up
the sides of the basin, of the glass
up fingers and hand and wrist

clinging to arm hair in mercurial bubbles
that detach and rise and join itself

the quick to heal
that wriggles up from hot
heat-wave pavement like teased hair

or has a wintry bite, or in the dog days saps
or is found at the bottom
of a mailbox on an empty house
or in a nest between twigs, among eggs

and we go on
with it within us
upon a dust speck
in bubble air

The Cenotaph

three idylls for Kenneth Koch

1   Moneses uniflora

Rain falls on the trash burning in an old oil drum and does not
     put it out.
It smoulders.
It is not because of the widely spaced big drops that the fire
     smoulders.
Garbage in the trash makes the fire smoulder. Banana peels, the
     thin skin in egg shells, sots, etc.
A thick white stench moves off not much higher than the rim
     of the oil drum into the woods to the stones.
The woods reek.
The stench stinks.
The fire mumbles its food.
It is not a successful combustion.
The dogs do not agree. The yellow dog and the red dog sniff at
     the drum as close as they can without burning their
     noses.
They lift legs against it and make a faint steam.
Then change places and as before.
That ends the ceremony so they run and bite each other's ears.
The oil drum is weathered in gritty stains of ember and urine.
The dark day thickens.
The rain falls heartily.
The fire indoors spits sparks and black and burning lumps are
     stamped out on the wood floor.
Others fall on the hearth and are left to their own devices.
Spruce wood, full of knots and resin.
Spruce wood burns quickly, and spits.

* 29
*

Is it less desirable than birch or apple?

Yes and no.

Or, that depends.

Not if you want a quick hot fire.

Besides, it is plentiful.

It abounds.

The woods smell sweetly of Parma violets from moneses uniflora,
      single flowered wintergreen

Trampled hay-scented fern and welcoming smoke.

The red dog comes in out of the rain to enact the chromo, *The
      Hound on the Hearth.*

He garners plaudits.

The chuck wood stove is too hot.

The hand on the dial in the door has passed five hundred and
      can go no higher.

Do not blame the quick hot spruce wood.

The under draft was left open.

The upper draft was left closed.

The fire burnt up in a rush.

Too hot an oven will ruin the meat thermometer.

Do not dash cold water on the red hot stove.

The iron will crack.

Today the sun came out.

Tonight we will not need a fire.

We eat aspic.

The incinerator oil drum is chock ablock with paint rags and
      newspapers soaked with turpentine.

The fire burns fiercely.

Its flames leap as high as the bending branches of the nearby
      birch.

The flames are seen but do not augment the sunlight.

If it is very hot it is still a local heat.

The dogs keep their distance.
The sun opens the flowers of the hawkweed.
Many are yellow and some are an orange red.
The hawkweed flowers are an idea about the color of fire.
The hawkweed are one thing and the fire is another.
If there is garbage in the fire it burns up too quickly to make a
    stink.
The fire is a hazard for the baby.
It is a good thing baby is fast asleep.
In the dark the biggest firefly is a cigarette.
The faint smell of burning is not faulty wiring.
It is the smell left by a hot day.

2   We see seals. Boats go by.

We see seals.
Boats go by.
The stones hurt tender feet, so we walk on hands.
It is easy: bodies are buoyant.
The water is clear.
It has thrown together some loose stones.
I lie on a water cushion and look down.
You lie on your back and look up.
The rocks have on seaweed.
We might slip on the weed and break my neck or at least sprain
    your ankle.
Salted nuts.
I have a red toenail.
It is red dye from orange socks bought in Vermont.
If sweat causes the sock to dye the nail red why won't the dye
    wash off of the nail?
It is incomprehensible.
I cannot understand it.

Some sunning seals swiftly slither and go plop.
Why?
A boat buzzed by.
The sea shapes the stones and dulls them.
Under and in it they shine colorfully.
It shows what it could do if it wished.
A final burnish is not its task.
Getting the most out of a stone might be to leave it alone.
There is nothing to eat except sea urchins and berries: blue and
        rasp.
There is nothing to drink except sea water full of trace elements.
That is not true.
There is a spring.
It is near here over there.
It is a good thing we did not bring the dog.
He might muddy the spring.
It is at the beach called The Beach Where the Indian Killed the
        Sheep.
A story about which I know nothing.
A title tells the tale.
Perhaps it is a tall tale.
It is certainly a dull one.
It is literary.
Did Beowulf call the sea, "the penis-shrinker"?
A seal sticks his snout out and gives a short snort.
The sun has got its ribbons snarled.
It is as bright on the other side as it is on this.
It is not like the moon which will rise between five and six and
        maunder among the spruce.
I am cold.
You are too.
We get out.
I dry off.

You sun.

I put on a sun-dried T shirt, shirt, undershorts, shorts, socks and
shoes.

Sneakers.

You dress too.

The way to the bog through the bog to the road from the south
to the north by the silver stile over no fence to the garden
by the apples to the gate to the lupines by the well to
the road and so home to lunch.

I lie down to read.

You canoe.

Do you know a camera that "costs $1,000.00 before accessories
is well worth it?"

Oh you do did you.

Someone is twelve years old and says putting a puzzle ring to-
gether is a "Herculanean task."

3   The Edge in the Morning

Walking to the edge with a cup of coffee

Sunup.

The sky is red.

Sunrise.

That way, the water is blinding.

That way, the water is dusted with sleep.

That way, the water shines as freshly as lead curling smoothly
under a knife.

The bay has a skin.

It swells it without breaking like water brimming in a glass.

On its skin and on mine the sun is warm.

The slipping air is thin and cold and cools the cup.

The coffee is cold.

Small fat gray brown birds in the grass bounce up from shadow
to shadow.

The false oats are ripened and bearded straw.
The sun strikes them.
They light up.
The quaking grass has collapsed in wire heaps.
It is not what it was.
The edges of the bay are thinnest at high tide.
It is low tide.
The seaweed has pods of air that are like coffee beans.
Out of the silence an engine approaches.
There are tide lines in the cup.
In the brilliance the boat is a dark chunk, bluntly whittled.
It steadily comes nearer.
It throbs.
It moves across the light and turns white.
It pays out two lines that fan and roll and add their action to
          the surface friction between air and water.
The bay is 1) a continuum and 2) change.
In the boat the figure of a man is ingeniously in scale.
A crow laughs.
The engine throttles.
The boat turns.
The ripples are twisted in a knot that shatters and dissolves.
The small turbulence breaks and melts.
The engine cuts to a rale.
The figure of a man turns, steps and bends and draws out of the
          dishonored and neglected grave cold blooded fury en-
          trapped in a lobster pot.
Carapace and claws snapping and thrashing, mottled stormily.
Gaudy shells packed with sweet meat.
The lobsterman turns toward you a face of weathered stone that
          cracks into a smile.
The price is up because the take is down.
He baits his trap and drops it in the sea.

The asthmatic purr chokes and resumes the stertorous breathing
   of normalcy.
The boat goes off to grow blue with distance.
The coffee cup has found its way onto the jut of a crag the
   size of a foot.
The little it holds is cold, bitter, gritty and tastes good.
The air has stopped sliding.
It is a breeze that is more like a wind.
It crumples the bay and stuffs it in a stone pocket.
The bay agitatedly tries to smooth itself out.
If it were tissue paper it would need damp and an iron.
It is a good deal more than damp.
What a lot of water.
A gull barks.
A baby barks back.
Three crows go by about their dark and iridescent business.
The sun is high enough to have its plain daily look of someone
   who takes in wash.
It dries the laundry.
Suppose I found a bone in the grass and told you it is one of
   Marc Bloch's?
It would not be true.
No it would not be true and the sea is not his grave.
Noble, great, and good:
It is his cenotaph.

After Joe Was at the Island

June 30, 1969

a good while after, on the upstairs east sleeping porch he used
for a studio, yellow petals—sharp yellow, shiny as lacquer—
caught in the tatters of a web, on the sill to the north, torn-out
book matches with burnt heads pointing all one way, laid in a
likeness of a woodpile (always making something); and a
pastryboard drawing board with edge of the paper color traces;
shades of sky up to white, of leaves and needles—All Sorts—
and not much smudged rose warming, the way grass in flower
sends a terra-cotta to slide through the unmown bending, the
given—the surface of the board—its woodenness abstracted
of brown pale skies, of agitated mud rising in an unreflecting
creek, of dry dirt and wet shingle—the tide is full only twice
a day and faded toward silver house shingles; or, shakes.

"Used Handkerchiefs 5¢"

Clean used ones, of course. Also a dresser scarf, woven with a
pattern of pansies looking alternately to right and to left; a
pillowcase full of carpet scraps; underdrawers of cambric with
an edging of tatting; black—shedding jet and bugles—crêpe,
as stuffed with dust and as damp, or as dry, as the wrinkled
hand of someone too old to die who dies because to wake up
this morning just slipped her mind; bent giant postcards: Mont
Pele and a fruitless wonderland of ice prisms, clear water-
diluted color chunks: blue; pink and green; sagging brown and
metal-threaded tapestry cloth within the gothic arch of a table
Motorola hiding a speaker from which once sped Flagstad's
more than melodious shriek and, over-enunciated as plums
wrapped in papers printed "Biscayne Farms," once trotted, like
a quick creek, the news that flaming passengers were falling
from the Hindenburg, a voice that left itself a small puddle
of kerosene on the linoleum; then there is your face, floating up
the stairs, big-eyed into the trash-and-treasures loft from which,
finally, dressed for tennis as you came, you go down again with
a find in hand: a slab of undyed linen its silverness yellowing
like a teaspoon from egg yolk, ironed with too cool an iron so
the washing crush marks make a pattern over the weave and,
above the thick welt of the hem, a cross-stitched border of
spruce and juniper unstylized (unless style is simply to choose)
in shades of drab that sink in, or emerge from: the hand
towel of today, embroidered forty some maybe years ago.

The Trash Book

for Joe Brainard

Then I do not know what
to paste next in the
Trash Book: grass, pretending
to be a smear maybe or
that stump there that knows
now it will never grow
up to be some pencils or
a yacht even. A piece of
voice saying (it sounds like)
"I thought her did." Or
the hum that hangs in only
my left ear. Or, "Beer" not
beer, all wet, the quiver
of the word one night in
1942 looking at a cardboard
girl sitting on a moon in
West Virginia. She smiled
and sipped her Miller's.

8/12/70

In early August among the spruce
fall parti-colored leaves
from random birch that hide
their crowns up toward the light—
deciduously needle-nested—
among the tumbled rocks—a
man-made scree below a house—
a dull green sumach blade
slashed with red clearer than
blood a skyblue red a first
fingertap, a gathering, a climax

Light from Canada

for Charles North

A wonderful freshness, air
that billows like bedsheets
on a clothesline and the clouds
hang in a traffic jam: summer
heads home. Evangeline,
our light is scoured and Nova
Scotian and of a clarity that
opens up the huddled masses
of the stolid spruce so you
see them in their bristling
individuality. The other
day, walking among them, I
cast my gaze upon the ground
in hope of orchids and,
pendant, dead, a sharp shadow
in the shade, a branch gouged
and left me "scarred forever
'neath the eye." Not quite. Not
the cut, but the surprise, and
how, when her dress caught fire,
Longfellow's wife spun
into his arms and in the dying

of its flaring, died. The
irreparable, which changes
nothing that went before
though it ends it. Above the wash
and bark of rumpled water, a gull
falls down the wind to dine
on fish that swim up to do same.

Gulls

Gulls
loudly insist on indefensible rights

Spruce
gather together on spindle shanks

Queen Anne's Lace
tip platters at perilous angles

Hawkweed
all sneeze at the same time

Rocks
go back to sleep

Birches
grunt as they scratch themselves

Stumps
grow old in hospitableness

Moss
free of dandruff

Bunchberries
trotting about

Closed Gentian Distances

A nothing day full of
wild beauty and the
timer pings. Roll up
the silver off the bay
take down the clouds
sort the spruce and
send to laundry marked,
more starch. Goodbye
golden- and silver-
rod, asters, bayberry
crisp in elegance.
Little fish stream
by, a river in water.

Fall
and
Winter

September

Swimming in the memorial
park pond smells of a dog

or just wading up and
down on trucked-in sand

oaks do their stuff
a dressy pine

and a kind of a mantid
that inspires respect

it isn't an insect with
only four legs when

its pincers snappily fold
back Danilova/Yastrezemski

that's it in September sun
two of its legs are like—you

know. Arms

Evening Wind

October hangs in grape
bunch lights among the leaves
of a giant tree whose leaves
are not unlike grape leaves:
a plane tree, or a sycamore?
The wind comes up the water
as water from a faucet
runs across a palm, the palm
of your hand, the water turned
on gently or broken into
cool molten wooly glass
by an aerator. And each
responds by his or its
own bending to it, tall tops
of hedge move all in a sideways
way, the grass (it begins
to have its matted resting
up for winter look) is freaked
by shade and quartz grit
bits of light, a pear tree
rocks at its roots and from
the eyebrow curves of branches
or under them flutters absurdly
its leaves like lashes. And I

am troubled by hatred for
the dead. Wind, you don't
blow hard enough, though
rising, in the smoky blue
of evening, mindless and in love.
Or would be if the wind
were not above such thoughts,
above thought, in fact
of course, though coursing,
cool as water, through it.

A Vermont Diary

November 1

> Slowly
> the dried up pond
> fills again. The blackish
> verge grows spongy. Packed
> with seeds of which some
> burst unseasonably into
> life: kinds of grass in
> tufted rays or with blades
> folded in purple cornucopias—
> low-growing bedstraw and
> others to you nameless—
> pushing out for room,
> radiating, starring the muck.
> A frail gray flower
> flies off, an insect
> that escaped the first
> combing frosts. It's
> not—"the fly buzzed"
> finding moods, reflectives:
> fall
> equals melancholy, spring,
> get laid: but to turn it all
> one way: in repetition, change:
> a continuity, the what
> of which you are a part.

The clouds are tinted
gray and violet and shred
the blue in other blues.
Each weed as you walk
becomes a rarity.

Quarter past four and evening turbulence begins, the sky
clotted with clouds, glazed and crazed like gray pottery.

It's warm for the time of year here—last night the Hal-
lowe'en weathercaster called it "living on borrowed time": last
year at this time there were five inches of snow ("On the
ground?" "No. In the trees.") 50° in Burlington (at 11 p.m.)—
51° in New York.

The hills that last year in early October I saw enflamed and
raging are now the browns and grays of lichened bark, the woods
lit by bare birch trunks and warmed by spruce and pine.

In a drugstore in Montpelier— "A bottle of Fitch Sham-
poo—" "Fix Shampoo? Is it got something special about it?"

November 2

The road goes down a steep gradient through the close har-
mony of the fields (frowsy with opening milkweed pods) and
there there is one larch, a pyramid of light among all that is
faded or bare or shroudedly evergreen.

From the ceiling comes a soft irregular scuffling—Joe mov-
ing his feet as he works—a fly at the window makes a dry re-

petitive nagging sound, like someone trying to start a car; and on the couch Whippoorwill, all wrapped up in himself, grunts and pulls himself a little tighter.

The light on the lake and trees beyond is wintry (though the day is warm), clear as water disclosing bare stems in a harsh chill. The light is colorless, harsh as an old photograph.

November 3

As the sun goes west the shadow of the ridge brings the pond to a reflecting black, its surface on the exposed side where the road goes round crinkled by the wind. The brush piles, stumps where they cleared dead elms, the harsh light, give it a raw frontier look: beyond the fact of beauty and the appearance of beauty, life's unrelenting hardness: ice broken, jammed, grinding on itself.

November 4
Antiquing: Hardwicke.

me—"We ought to change 'Kill a cop tonight: Hallowe'en,' to 'Ball your local sheriff.'"
Joe—"Why? Is she cute?"

Thinking about Larry Fagin—"Then I went home and had this wonderful dream."

November 5

Kenward is right behind me taking wood ashes out of the fireplace to add to the compost. Actually, he is through doing that and is laying a fire, bringing big chunks of wood up from the cellar. Whippoorwill hops off the couch with a sneeze and gallops after him, then comes back to lie in some unexpected sunshine. Up until now—noon—it's been almost a snow-bearing sky, though still very warm for November, with clouds nothing like fog over the further hills, but now the middle of the sky is smeared and worn through and some pallid light makes weak shadows along the road.

> Fine lines, so many lines,
> lines on lines, the hills
> are all a haze of twigs—
>
> the armatures of summer,
> lichens on the trunks,
> are whitely acid green—

November 6

Not quite four o'clock and all heavily, snowily overcast, except down the valley in the south there is a clear strip of sky, the pale green of an unripe peach. A couple of hours ago, when I went for a nice long walk, the sky was a most tender blue—a French blue, like the sky was over Cherbourg one morning— seventeen years ago. A sky of rain clouds that morning was breaking up and the pilot boat that brought the immigration officers out bounced in heavy seas. I remember a woman in a transparent hooded raincoat sprinkled with raindrops.

My walk—the road goes steeply downhill between fields, then winds through the woods beside a stream which makes several waterfalls. Down and down, past a cleared place full of stumps where timber was cut last year and a hunter's car was parked today. Then the road levels off, a scrubby wet looking field opens on the left, and at the end of it is Farmer Martin's house, where Emslie Road ends in a right angle to the road that goes from Maple Corner to East Calais. The Martins' house, which is of a nice old kind (Cape Cod) but in need of a good deal more than paint, is built in what must always have been a rather odd place—so low and damp in the creek flats, and likely to flood in the spring—one wonders what the inducement was to build there—not well water, in these gushing hills—that it was on a road, and the richness of the bottom land along the creek? Little use seems made of it now. There's always a lot of junk piled up beside the house—lately including a white toilet—and one window was propped open by a tin can. And what was once a chicken run has a rank harvest of sere thistles.

I took the right-hand turn, a long gradient that must take one up again as high as the house (well, two-thirds) and twice the length, a much easier ascent than going up the road down Apple Hill, but enough to work up a sweat. In thin woods facing south many more ferns still are green than up here, and in a growing up field old apple trees still hold a lot of fruit, yellow, or soft orange-red, and one a brilliant red, like rose hips. A lot of the land is posted, but one man's said hunting was permitted by request, and gave his phone number.

Rather a relief when the road levels out at Kent's Corners—the old brick tavern, shuttered for the winter, looking a good deal more four-square on the outside than it does inside. All the houses on this stretch of a mile or less are nicely kept up—especially the one at the first crossroads, where they keep guinea fowl (polka dots!) and there is a stream which in September is thick with forget-me-nots. A week ago this road was all churned up, but has now been leveled and rolled. A couple of big yellow dump trucks passed me going back and forth with loads of fill, which a huge complicated machine was pushing into place in front of the Co-Op at Maple Corner. The part of the Montpelier Road that comes down a short steep hill there is going to be paved—or at least, straightened. Another right-hand turn there, through the hamlet, past the school and Marian Anderson the postmistress's house and the dairy farm and its close-cropped, stony, uphill pastures. Two shaggy horses with heavy rumps were standing around looking solemn, and a lot of long clouds like old-fashioned trolley cars were going along overhead, some kind of osier was a vineyard beside the road and I thought, I wouldn't want anything to be different about this day—a sudden wonderful feeling of accepting things as they are, even the things you don't like—the plain Jane new houses, or a rough-looking dog that shot out, fiercely barking at me as I passed a garage—scary, even though chained. At the top of the rise, in the shade of some trees beside a road to a field, there was a little snow left from last night's flurries, which had been rather hard to believe in earlier, under the blue, and where this road turns off I saw through the leafless trees a pond, straight down below the fields, I never knew was there before.

November 7

A Gray Thought

In the sky a gray thought
ponders on three kinds of green:
Brassy tarnished leaves of lilacs
holding on half-heartedly and long
after most turned and fell to make
a scatter rug, warmly, brightly brown.
Odd, that the tattered heart-shapes
on a Persian shrub should stay
as long as the northern needles

of the larch. Near, behind the lilac
on a trunk, pale Paris green
as moonlight, growing on another time scale
a slowness becoming vast as though
all the universe were an atom
of a filterable virus in a head
that turns an eye to smile
or frown or stare into other
eyes: and not of gods, but creatures
whose size begins beyond the sense of size:
lichens, softly colored, hard in durance,
a permanence like rock on a transient tree.
And another green, a dark thick green
to face the winter, laid in layers on
the spruce and balsam or in foxtail
bursts on pine in springy shapes
that weave and pierce
the leafless and unpatterned woods.

Later.

Verge

A man cuts brush
and piles it
for a fire where
fireweed will flower
maybe, one day.
All the leaves
are down except
the few that aren't.
They shake or

a wind shakes
them but they
won't go oh
no there goes
one now. No.
It's a bird
batting by.
The small lake,
shrunk, shivers
like a horse
twitching off
flies. Flies
drunkenly stagger
between window
and storm sash.
They hatch, lay,
buzz and die.
The sky grows
gray, goes pale,
bears a whitlow
or splits and
shows a lining
light sea green.
But the lake
is black. Back
of the trees
are other trees
where deer stoop
and step and
the independent skunk
securely waddles.
An unseen

something stirs
and says: No
snow yet but
it will snow.
The trees sneeze:
You bet it
will, compiling
a white and wordless
dictionary
in which brush
cut, piled and
roofed with glitter
will catch and burn
transparently
bright in white
defining "flame."
So long, north.
See you later
in other weather.

Late afternoon.

Another sky that looked snow-bearing breaks up and sunlight falls hit or miss on the hills.

Country living. The Pyrofax (the gas which the stove burns) began to give out the day before yesterday (you can tell it's running out when you begin to smell it: spooky). So Kenward went to the Co-Op and called for new tanks, which were to come that afternoon or, at the latest, yesterday. Still no Pyrofax.

Tomorrow we return to New York, a long drive, and the next night, a big birthday party (mine).

A Stone Knife

Dear Kenward,
                    What a pearl
of a letter knife. It's just
the thing I needed, something
to rest my eyes on, and always
wanted, which is to say
it's that of which I
felt the lack but
didn't know of, of no
real use and yet
essential as a button
box, or maps, green
morning skies, islands and
canals in oatmeal, the steam
off oyster stew. Brown
agate, veined as a woods
by smoke that has to it
the watery twist of eel grass
in a quick, rust-discolored
cove. Undulating lines of
northern evening—a Munch
without the angst—a
hint of almost amber:
to the nose, a resinous

thought, to the eye, a
lacquered needle green
where no green is, a
present after-image.
Sleek as an ax, bare
and elegant as a tarn,
manly as a lingam,
November weather petrified,
it is just the thing
to do what with? To
open letters? No, it
is just the thing, an
object, dark, fierce
and beautiful in which
the surprise is that
the surprise, once
past, is always there:
which to enjoy is
not to consume. The un-
recapturable returns
in a brown world
made out of wood,
snow streaked, storm epi-
center still in stone.

The Dog Wants His Dinner

for Clark Coolidge

The sky is pitiless. I beg
your pardon? OK then
the sky is pitted. The yard
is sand and laced with roots
afloat on rock encasing fire.
You think so do you. No.
Yes. Don't know. Check one.
Forget all you ever knew.
Sorry. Not my romance. What
is? Sorry. We don't take
in trick questions. You mean?
I do: put down that.
Put that down too. Skies
of spit, seas where whales
piss and die to make a bar
of scented soap, uhm smells
good. She came in like an ex-
cited headline. The deer
they all were starving! To
death, even, perhaps. And
eating people! What to do
with these disordered herds
of words? I said I would
eat my words and do so, now
you see. He eats them, all

up. Greedily. Yesterday the
air was squeaky clean today
it's dull and lifeless as an
addict's armpit. Surely you
mean leafless. I have a flea
bite, here, pink, of course
as an eye disease: the cat
who brings me fleas dies
like a dog, sleepily, or
an unwatered plant. That
was exciting wasn't it. It's
not that I crave. Uh did
you say crave? Some words
are briefly worse than others:
get the Librium gun and point
it and the Kodak at that Kodiak.
You see? No hope. So don't
hope. Hop, skip, jump or
lie down. Feed your face.
Now feed the dog. He ate his.
He is eating the cat who
objects. Fix the fire. Put
out the light. An ice cold
hand slides in the window
to touch your uncovered head
forehead cheeks lips lobes
and all with worlds of fire
chilled by distance. O night.
Bedclothes loosen. Unseen twigs
erect themselves in air. You
asleep too, O magic root.

Running Footsteps

A thin brown stain
down the white brick wall
I guess yes
the new roof leaks
and there are holes
drilled in the asphalt
out there where manhole
covers used to blow:
escape for leaks. Sleet
down the chimney:
a rustle broken
into dots and dashes. Then
a midwinter downpour.
The streets are rivers
or the water streets
in a smalltown dream
"They live on Water Street
near the corner of Front Street
off Railroad Avenue."
The current fails.
Lights go out
in parts of town. In
the slosh there are
running footsteps: has
got to go though
an act of clouds would will

otherwise. Otherwise,
had stayed where was . . . ?
Couldn't. Why?
On and off lights
prolong into surges
the chatter of
rain on rain, the up
close rats' nesting noise
in the chimney: "It's
a good night to stay
in" so out you
go into it it's
almost like
that other night
you left holding
your breath to
descend and issue
screaming: your
tonight running
footsteps, rain
icy and loud
is a kind of
what to your
surprise is you
screaming in
fear, in rage,
instinctual
to find relief
muscular surges
running footsteps
the rain
rain-chilled
to be alive

The Crystal Lithium

The smell of snow, stinging in nostrils as the wind lifts it from
    a beach
Eye-shuttering, mixed with sand, or when snow lies under the
    street lamps and on all
And the air is emptied to an uplifting gassiness
That turns lungs to winter waterwings, buoying, and the bright
    white night
Freezes in sight a lapse of waves, balsamic, salty, unexpected:
Hours after swimming, sitting thinking biting at a hangnail
And the taste of the—to your eyes—invisible crystals irradiates
    the world
"The sea is salt"
"And so am I"
"Don't bite your nails"
                    and the metal flavor of a nail—are these
    brads?—
Taken with a slight spitting motion from between teeth and
    whanged into place
(Boards and sawdust) and the nail set is ridged with cold
Permanently as marble, always degrees cooler than the rooms of
    air it lies in
Felt as you lay your cheek upon the counter on which sits a
    blue-banded cup
A counter of condensed wintry exhalations glittering
    infinitesimally
A promise, late on a broiling day in late September, of the cold
    kiss

Of marble sheets to one who goes barefoot quickly in the snow
and early
Only so far as the ash can—bang, dump—and back and slams
the door:
Too cold to get up though at the edges of the blinds the sky
Shows blue as flames that break on a red sea in which black
coals float:
Pebbles in a pocket embed the seam with grains of sand
Which, as they will, have found their way into a pattern between
foot and bedfoot
"A place for everything and everything in its place" how
wasteful, how wrong
It seems when snow in fat, hand-stuffed flakes falls slow and
steady in the sea
"Now you see it, now you don't" the waves growl as they grind
ashore and roll out
At your feet (in boots) a Christmas tree naked of needles
Still wound with swags of tarnishing tinsel, faintly alarming as
the thought
Of damp electricity or sluggish lightning and for your health
desiring pains
The wind awards: Chapped Lips: on which to rub Time's latest
acquisition
Tinned, dowel shaped and inappropriately flavored sheep wool
fat
A greasy sense-eclipsing fog "I can't see
Without my glasses" "You certainly can't see with them all
steamed up
Like that. Pull over, park and wipe them off." The thunder of a
summer's day
Rolls down the shimmering blacktop and mowed grass juice
thickens the air
Like "Stir until it coats the spoon, remove from heat, let cool and
chill"

Like this, graying up for more snow, maybe, in which a small flock
Of—sparrows?—small, anyway, dust kitty-colored birds fly up
On a dotted diagonal and there, ah, is the answer:
Starlings, bullies of birdland, lousing up
The pecking order, respecters of no rights (what bird is) unloved (oh?)
Not so likeable as some: that's temperate enough and the temperature
Drops to rise to snowability of a softness even in its scent of roses
Made of untinted butter frosting: Happy Name Day, Blue Jay, staggering
On slow-up wings into the shrunk into itself from cold forsythia snarl
And above these thoughts there waves another tangle but one parched with heat
And not with cold although the heat is on because of cold settled all
About as though, swimming under water, in clearly fishy water, you
Inhaled and found one could and live and also found you altogether
Did not like it, January, laid out on a bed of ice, disgorging
February, shaped like a flounder, and March with her steel bead pocketbook,
And April, goofy and under-dressed and with a loud laugh, and May
Who will of course be voted Miss Best Liked (she expects it),
And June, with a toothpaste smile, fresh from her flea bath, and gross July,
Flexing itself, and steamy August, with thighs and eyes to match, and September
Diving into blue October, dour November, and deadly dull December which now

* 67
*

And then with a surprised blank look produces from its hand the
    ace of trumps
Or sets within the ice white hairline of a new moon the gibbous
    rest:
Global, blue, Columbian, a blue dull definite and thin as the
    first day
Of February when, in the steamed and freezing capital cash
    built
Without a plan to be its own best monument its skyline set in
    stacks
Like poker chips (signed, "Autodidact"), at the crux of a view
    there crosses
A flatcar-trailer piled with five of the cheaper sort of yachts,
    tarpaulined,
Plus one youth in purple pants, a maid in her uniform and an
    "It's not real
Anything" Cossack hat and coat, a bus one-quarter full of
    strangers and
The other familiar fixings of lengthening short days: "He's
    outgrown them
Before you can turn around" and see behind you the landscape
    of the past
Where beached boats bask and terraced cliffs are hung with
    oranges
Among dark star-gleaming leaves, and, descending the dizzying
    rough stairs
Littered with goat turd beads—such packaging—you—he—
    she—
One—someone—stops to break off a bit of myrtle and recite all
    the lines
Of Goethe that come back, and those in French, "*Connais-tu*
    . . . ?" the air
Fills with chalk dust from banged erasers, behind the February
    dunes

Ice boats speed and among the reeds there winds a little frozen
stream
Where kids in kapok ice-skate and play at Secret City as the sun
Sets before dinner, the snow on fields turns pink and under the
hatched ice
The water slides darkly and over it a never before seen
liquefaction of the sun
In a chemical yellow greener than sulphur a flash of petroleum
by-product
Unbelievable, unwanted and as lovely as though someone you
knew all your life
Said the one inconceivable thing and then went on washing
dishes: the sky
Flows with impersonal passion and loosening jet trails (eyes
tearing from the cold)
And on the beach, between foam frozen in a thick scalloped
edging so like
Weird cheek-mottling pillowcase embroidery, on the
water-darkened sand the waves
Keep free of frost, a gull strangles on a length of nylon fishline
and the dog
Trots proudly off, tail held high, to bury a future dinner among
cut grass on a dune:
The ice boats furl their sails and all pile into cars and go off to
the super market
Its inviting foods and cleansers sold under tunes with sealed in
memory-flavor
"Hot House Rhubarb" "White Rock Girl" "Citrus Futures" "Cheap
Bitter Beans" and
In its parking lot vast as the kiss to which is made the most
complete surrender
In a setting of leaves, backs of stores, a house on a rise admired
for being

Somewhat older than some others (prettier, too?) a man in a
    white apron embraces a car
Briefly in the cold with his eyes as one might hug oneself for
    warmth for love
—What a paint job, smooth as an eggplant; what a meaty chest,
    smooth as an eggplant
—Is it too much to ask your car to understand you? the converse
    isn't and the sky
Maps out new roads so that, driving at right angles to the wind,
    clouds in ranks
Contrive in diminishing perspective a part of a picture postcard
    of a painting
Over oak scrub where a filling station has: gas, a locked toilet
    (to keep dirt in)
A busted soda pop machine, no maps and "I couldn't tell you
    thet" so
The sky empties itself to a color, there, where yesterday's puddle
Offers its hospitality to people-trash and nature-trash in tans and
    silvers
And black grit like that in corners of a room in this or that cheap
    dump
Where the ceiling light burns night and day and we stare at or
    into each
Other's eyes in hope the other reads there what he reads: snow,
    wind
Lifted; black water, slashed with white; and that which is, which
    is beyond
Happiness or love or mixed with them or more than they or less,
    unchanging change,
"Look," the ocean said (it was tumbled, like our sheets), "look
    in my eyes"

Loving
You

Janis Joplin's Dead:
Long Live Pearl

"Ever write any love poems?"

you call:
guarded voices. O
Commodore
Hotel, I like
free speech. "Free-
dom's just
a word." I bet
you think
I'm giving you
the old
McGee. I
ain't givin'
you nothin',
Buster: just
walk on in
and help yourself.
Set right down
and rap a while.
Take a toke.
Take two. Do
your thing. I'm puttin' on
Pearl (O Pearl) and
The In White Wrappers
(groovy group)
or *Company.* Couldn't
care
less. Not

true. Then
dig right
in and help yourself. You think
I don't mean it? Not
on your Kodachrome. Or
it's
a put on? Maybe
baby: that's
a game that two
can play
at: in fact it
takes two
and only two:
                    "holdin' "

"body
next to
mine"

Eyes

seta cangiante
eyes that change
changeable as changeable
silk, silk that
refracts
as bearer walks
in sunlight
into shade
from Piazza, say,
San Marco
into suncharged
shadowy arcade
or under trees
green, green
and between
blue, blue, blue
bluest blue
eyes of un-
weavable color
human eyes, man
size : unsilken
reflections :
hazel, gray-
blue, 'tea
ashes' Chinese,

ordinary eyes:
The Big Salty,
shifting restless,
under overcast:
smile, cold, half-
asleep
and deep in August
grass, elms, weeping
birches and all
green, too
green, so green
and the eyes
pick it up and
flash *il raggio verde*
the green ray
al tramonto
sunset flash
the red
reversal: i.e.
green

And in your eyes
your suddenly so
green eyes
the flash holds
steadily and
you smile or
I hope so: it
is not August
yet, *Occhi*
di seta cangiante
mi segue?

The Night

The night is filled with indecisions
To take a downer or an upper
To take a walk
To lie
Down and relax

I order you: RELAX

To face the night
Alight—or dark—the air
Conditioner
The only song:
I love you so
Right now I need you so
So tired and so upset
And yet I musn't phone:
I didn't know
I touched a wound that never healed
A trauma: wounds will heal
And all I did
Was panic so briefly
On the phone
"Oh baby! you scared me."
No, what you said
First on the phone

Was, "Baby, I'll be right there."
You were. You did. You
Came, it seemed, as fast
As light, you love me so.
I didn't know someone
Once hurt you so,
Went suicidal: head in the oven
Threat—that
Hysteria bit. Not
My trip.
I am not suicidal:
We are strong and
You know it and
Yet
I must sleep
And wait—I
    love you so
You will know
I know you do
Already know:
We love each other
So. Good night
My own, my love
My dear, my dearest dear
It's true
We do we
Love each
Other so

Like Lorraine Ellison

Zéphyrine Drouhin
lines out her
Cerise Magic
in pear tree shade:
back-up group, The Persian
Double Yellows (gone,
about, over). And through the snares
sexily come saxes: through
solid shadow-green
of brushing leaves, clear
as a blues, violet sage,
flowering saxes. I
send you all the love
("Who's Zéphyrine?"
in the world
("She was a somebody
or would
(once, now
if it were mine
(she is
to
(a rose"
give

Letter to a Friend:
Who Is Nancy Daum?

All things are real
no one a symbol:
curtains (shantung
      silk)
potted palm, a
bust: flat, with pipe—
  M. Pierre Martory
a cut-out by Alex
          Katz:
Dreaming eyes
        and pipe
Contiguous to
en terre cuite
          Marie
Antoinette
her brown and seeming
living curls
and gaze seen as
Reverie: *My Lady*
of My Edgeworth
("Prince Albert in
the can?" "Better
let him out, I . . .")
pipe dream. Some
Vitamins; more
Flying Buzzard
      ware:

a silver chain—my
silver chain
from Denmark from
you by way
of London—
(I put it on: cold
and I love
its weight:
   argento
      pessante)
a *sang de boeuf*
     spitoon
or Beauty bowl,
a compact
with a Red Sea
    scene
holding little
pills (Valium
for travel strain),
this French
   lamp
whose stem of
  glass
Lights softly
        up
entwined with
autumn trees
(around the base
   are reeds)
its glass shade
   slightly oiled
as is the dawn
above a swamp
lagoon or fen where

hunters lurk and
down *marc* or *cognac*
or home-made rotgut
of their choice,
I—have lost
my place:
No, here it is:
Traherne,
Poems, Centuries
and Three
Thanksgivings,
a book beneath
the notebook
in which I write.
Put off the light—
the French lamp
(signed, somewhere)
And put it on:
the current
flows.
My heart
beats. Nerves,
muscles,
the bright invisible
red blood—*sang*
d'homme
helps (is
that the word?)
propel
this ball-point
pen:
black ink is
not black
blood.

Two other books:
The Gay
      Insider
—good—*Run*
Little Leather
Boy awaits
assessment
on my Peter Meter.
A trove of glass
   within a
   cabinet
near my
     knees
I wish I were on
my knees
embracing
   yours
      my cheek
against the suiting of
         whatever
suit—about now—
or soon, or late—
("I'm not prompt"
   you said, rueful
        factual
"I" I said, "climb
walls")
O Day!
  literal
and unsymbolic
      day:
silken: gray: sunny:
   in salt and pepper
tweed soot storm:

* 83
    *

guide, guard,
          be freely
                    pierced
by the steel and
gold-eyed
needle passes—stitches
—of my love, my
                    lover,
                              our love,
his lover—I
                    am he—
          (is not
at any tick
each and every life
at hazard: *faites
vos jeux,*
          messieurs)
. . . Where am I?
          en route to
                    a literal
Vermont. It's
                    time
                              to
—oh, do this
          do that—.
I'll call.
Perhaps we'll
     lunch? We
already
said goodbye a
long farewell
for a few weeks'
          parting!
My ocean liner,
     I am your

tug. "Life
is a bed
      of roses:
rugosas,
nor is it always
    summer."
Goodbye. Hello.
        Kiss
Hug. I
  gotta
run. Pierre
Martory,
his semblance,
smokes a St.
      Simonian
pipe and thinks
Mme. de Sévigné
-type thoughts.
He was, when
     posing,
perhaps, projecting
A Letter to a Friend.
      (signed)—
all my
—you know—
    ton
       Dopey.
PS The lamp is
  signed, Daum,
    Nancy.
Hence I surmise
    she made
or, at least,
     designed it.
Who *is* Nancy Daum?

Letter poem #2

Riding along in the beautiful day (there go two
blue enamel silos), half-reading about marvelous
Chamfort, thinking of "my own, my dearest," and
among other you thoughts—

> White clouds in blue above the birches
> You too are like my head, filled with
> And adrift in love, which is the sap
> That rises, stiffening these trees

We Are Leaves

There are leaves
there are trees
there is a tuba vine
"she"—a voice
she sings in other
words than what
disc grooves carry:
your name your face
our privacy in
hotel rooms with
cheap vodka cheap
quinine water our
nights are days
the morning comes
and goes and we
are pleased or
"who cares?" We
saw that view
of shimmering tall
offices. Today.
Today is muggy
gray—I don't
mind: why care?
Today you see
another view

desk and win-
dow ledge, while
mine—my view
that is—is
window ledge
and desk. Do
I miss you?
You know, yes
and I know,
no, you are
so with me
when apart, I
think I under-
stand you and
you me: I'm
happy as a rained
on leaf or
lettuce in a
crisper. You
love me and I
reciprocate.
The leaves—
it's almost
fall—look
to last for
ever—they will
come tumbling
down. I'm glad
we are not
leaves, or even
trees whose twigs
mesh. We are—

you are you,
I am I, and
we mesh. And
to ourselves
we speak our
thoughts and
touch and that
is love, isn't
it? What Doc
called, Gen-
ital contact.
And lighter
than a zeppelin
the sense of
touch brushed
lightly one
against the other
we two, together
here among leaves

*

Await

The scars upon the day
are harsh marks of
tranquility. I scarcely
know where you are:
awake? After lunch, a
Sunday snooze? Is
the ivy weeded yet?
Let the frost do
it its way. Smile, my
dear my dandy, when
you see this. That's
not much to ask, though
no smile on order
is quite the spontaneous
real thing. The day
grinds to a halt all
dusk and yellow rose.
What's a hundred some
miles or so? Or—let's
see—fifty hours?
Time of all things
is most variable, a
seed you plant to see
what in the world
it is a seed of: time,
hours compressed into
a kiss, a lick, or
stretched out by a

train into an endless
rubber band. All we
know is that for such
as us it is not end-
less: is time too to
be found of an atomic
structure? I
would be the last to
know, busily waiting
to see and smile
as you smile and bend
to kiss. Why soon it
will be only forty
nine hours, cubed in-
visibly like the sec-
tions of a creek.
A record spins,
these keys go clack
why soon I'll see
you and soon you'll
see me. I can enjoy
the here and now
but, wind shivering
clear day, I live
and love to anticipate
my hands on you and
yours on me, the
hours flow by and
a white gull is
black against
November evening
light, expressed,
it seems, from
late yellow grapes.

Steaming Ties

Steaming ties, cutting rue
when I'm alone it's hard
at times to know how unalone
I am, loved by you. We phone.
A heavy talk on real estate, you
own land. I don't. Once did.
Sold it for a trip
Italy, France, two years:
bye bye, Arkansas homestead.
Still and all on this radiant
September leaf light day
the leaves lit it seems or
seeming is from insides,
lovely inwardness of leaves
that dapple themselves with shade,
and all, and still I have a
place to lay my head
on you, oh, anywhere:
I'm no body bigot but
sometimes even yet or now, I
mean, I forget for a few
sad minutes how unalone I
am, steaming ties you gave
me, ties are, yes even ties,
are silk and real. Your

voice to me is silk and rustles.
We will meet, soon, not
soon enough. I remember I'm
unalone, you are with me,
salty sneezes off Atlantic
Ocean, there, where you are
here, in my heart and head
you blend in softly bright
September: you are moonrise
you are pain, you're mine
and I am yours, steaming
out silk ties, they bind

Watching You

Watching you sleep
a thing you do so well
no shove no push
on the sliding face
of sleep as on
the deep a sea bird
of a grand wingspread
trusts what it knows
and I who rumple crumple
and mash (snore) amble
and ankle about wide
awake, wanting to fold,
loving to watch sleep
embodied in you my
warm machine that draws
me back to bed
and you who turn
all toward me
to love and seduce
me back to sleep "You
said 9:30, now it's
10:" you just
don't seem to care
cold coffee (sugar,
no milk) about time:

you never do, never
get roiled the way
I do "Should I nag
you or shut up? If
you say, I will"
always be
glad to return to
that warm turning
to me in that
tenderest moment
of my nights,
and more, my days.

Letter Poem #3

The night is quiet
as a kettle drum
the bull frog basses
tuning up. After
swimming, after sup-
per, a Tarzan movie,
dishes, a smoke. One
planet and I
wish. No need
of words. Just
you, or rather,
us. The stars tonight
in pale dark space
are clover flowers
in a lawn the expanding
Universe in which
we love it is
our home. So many
galaxies and you my
bright particular,
my star, my sun, my
other self, my bet-
ter half, my one

**About
the
Author**

James Schuyler was born in Chicago in 1933. He
was formerly on the staff of the Museum of Modern
Art, and an associate editor of *Art News,* to which he
continues to contribute articles. Aside from his
poems, collected in *Freely Espousing,* he is the author
of two novels: *Alfred and Guinevere* and, with John
Ashbery, *A Nest of Ninnies.* He has recently received
a creative writing grant from the National Council
on the Arts. Mr. Schuyler makes his home in New
York City and in Southampton, Long Island.

.